## Animal Homes

# A Termite's Colony

Arthur Best

New York

Published in 2019 by Cavendish Square Publishing, LLC
243 5th Avenue, Suite 136, New York, NY 10016

Copyright © 2019 by Cavendish Square Publishing, LLC

First Edition

No part of this publication may be reproduced, stored in a retrieval system, or transmitted in any form or by any means—electronic, mechanical, photocopying, recording, or otherwise—without the prior permission of the copyright owner. Request for permission should be addressed to Permissions, Cavendish Square Publishing, 243 5th Avenue,
Suite 136, New York, NY 10016. Tel (877) 980-4450; fax (877) 980-4454.

Website: cavendishsq.com

This publication represents the opinions and views of the author based on his or her personal experience, knowledge, and research. The information in this book serves as a general guide only. The author and publisher have used their best efforts in preparing this book and disclaim liability rising directly or indirectly from the use and application of this book.

All websites were available and accurate when this book was sent to press.

Library of Congress Cataloging-in-Publication Data

Title: A termite's colony / Arthur Best.
Description: New York : Cavendish Square, 2019. | Series: Animal homes | Includes index.
Identifiers: ISBN 9781502636768 (pbk.) | ISBN 9781502636744 (library bound) | ISBN 9781502636775 (6 pack) | ISBN 9781502636751 (ebook)
Subjects: LCSH: Termites--Juvenile literature. | Animals--Habitations--Juvenile literature.
Classification: LCC QL529.B48 2019 | DDC 595.7'36--dc23

Editorial Director: David McNamara
Copy Editor: Rebecca Rohan
Associate Art Director: Amy Greenan
Designer: Megan Metté
Production Coordinator: Karol Szymczuk
Photo Research: J8 Media

The photographs in this book are used by permission and through the courtesy of: Cover Inc/Shuterstock.com; p. 5 PK289/Shutterstock.com; p. 7 Piotr Naskrecki/Minden Pictures/Getty Images; p. 9 Superoke/Shutterstock.com; p. 11 PK6289/iStock/Thinkstock; p. 13 Sanya Muangkotr/Shutterstock.com; p. 15 Chakkrachai Nicharat/Shutterstock.com; p. 17 ©iStockphoto.com/PDQ1000; p. 19 Sydeen/Shutterstock.com; p. 21 Janelle Lugge/Shuterstock.com.

Printed in the United States of America

# Contents

A Termite's Home ............. **4**

New Words .................... **22**

Index ........................... **23**

About the Author ........... **24**

Termites are bugs.

They look like ants.

But they have soft bodies.

5

Termites live in groups.

These groups are called **colonies**.

Many termites live in a colony.

Termites eat dead plants.

They eat dead trees.

They eat a lot!

9

Termites make their homes.

Their homes are called nests.

Some termites live in wood.

They eat into the wood.

They make their home bigger!

Some termites live in the ground.

They dig.

They make **tunnels**.

Termites can make big **mounds**.

The mounds are made from **soil**.

They can be taller than a person!

17

Each termite has a job.

Some termites find food.

Some build the nest.

Some **protect** it.

19

Termites work together.

They make amazing homes!

21

# New Words

**colonies** (KAHL-uh-neez) Groups of termites.

**mounds** (MOUNDZ) Piles.

**protect** (pro-TEKT) Keep safe.

**soil** (SOYL) Dirt.

**tunnels** (TUN-ulz) Paths under the ground.

# Index

colonies, 6

ground, 14

mounds, 16

nests, 10, 18

protect, 18

soil, 16

tunnels, 14

wood, 12

# About the Author

**Arthur Best** lives in Wisconsin with his wife and son. He has written many other books for children. He has seen termites in dead trees.

## About BOOKWORMS

Bookworms help independent readers gain reading confidence through high-frequency words, simple sentences, and strong picture/text support. Each book explores a concept that helps children relate what they read to the world they live in.